GUIDE TO THE BLUE TONGUE

GUIDE TO THE BLUE TONGUE

POEMS BY VIRGIL SUÁREZ

University of Illinois Press
Urbana and Chicago

∞ This book is printed on acid-free paper.

Library of Congress Cataloging-in-Publication Data
Suárez, Virgil, 1962–
Guide to the blue tongue : poems / by Virgil Suárez.
p.   cm.
ISBN 0-252-02734-5 (cloth : acid-free paper)
ISBN 0-252-07050-X (paper : acid-free paper)
1. Cuban Americans—Poetry. 2. Cuba—Poetry. I. Title.
PS3569.U18G85   2002
811'.54—dc21   2001004330

ACKNOWLEDGMENTS

Grateful acknowledgment is made to the editors and publishers of the following journals in which some of these poems first appeared, sometimes in a slightly different form: *Abiko Quarterly* (Japan), *American Scholar, Amethyst Review* (Canada), *Antigonish Review* (Canada), *Artful Dodge, Artword Quarterly, Atlanta Review, Aura Literary Arts Review, Barnwood Review, Beloit Poetry Journal, Bloomsbury Review, Blue Mesa Review, Blue Sofa, Café Review, Caribbean Writer, Chariton Review, Chelsea, Comstock Review, Confrontation, Contemporary Verse* (Canada), *Controlled Burn, Crab Creek Review, Cream City Review, Denver Quarterly, English Journal, Faultline, Fiddlehead* (Canada), *5AM, Florida Review, Gaspereau Review* (Canada), *Gulf Coast, Hampden Sydney Review, Harpweaver* (Canada), *Hunger Magazine, Illuminations, Imago* (Australia), *Indiana Review, International Poetry Review, Iron Horse Literary Review, The Journal, Louisiana Literature, Meridian, Michigan Quarterly Review, Mid-American Review, New Letters, Northwest Review, Notre Dame Review, Pacific Coast Journal, Poems and Plays, Poet Lore, Poetry London* (UK), *Poetry Wales* (UK), *Portland Review, Prairie Schooner, Rattapallax, River City, River Styx, Seam* (UK), *Sonora Review, Southern Poetry Review, Southwest Review, Sycamore Review, Texas Review, TriQuarterly, Underwood Review, Water and Stone, Wavelength,* and *Witness.* "Prospero's Papermaking Recipe" was featured on the *Poetry Daily* Web site with a different title.

I would also like to express my deepest gratitude to Ryan G. Van Cleave for his generous help with revision. Also for their support and inspiration I say thank you to the following poets: Jeff Knorr, Gaylord Brewer, Bob Hicok, J. J. Blickstein, Hayan Charara, Margot Schilpp, Timothy Liu, Jim Barnes, Luci

Tapahonso, Jim Daniels, Jarret Keene, Todd J. Pierce, Wasabi Kanastoga, Toi Derricote, Gustavo Pérez Firmat, Adrian C. Louis, Bruce Weigl, Naomi Shihab Nye, Denise Duhamel, Kim Addonizio, E. Ethelbert Miller, Reginald Gibbons, Laure-Anne Bosselaar, Sherman Alexie, Yusef Komunyakaa, Dorianne Laux, and Nick Carbó.

Very special thanks go to Laurence Lieberman not only for the inspiration provided by his rich poetry of the Caribbean but also for his astute and much-needed editorial wisdom. Without his vision and guidance this book would not exist. Also, as always, thanks to my wife and daughter for the love and support.

Many of these poems were written with the generous support of a National Endowment of the Arts fellowship.

For R.G.V.C.

El Boppier

&

For all my students

Soy un ajiaco de contradicciones,
un puré de impurezas:
a little square from Rubik's Cuba
que nadie nunca acoplará.
(Cha-cha-cha.).
—Gustavo Pérez Firmat, "Bilingual Blues"

THREE — BLUE TONGUE POEMS

ONE — *MASCARAS* / MASKS

In this bare island by your spell . . .
Let your indulgence set me free.
—Prospero

SON MONTUNO

Some call this rapture of wind against the fronds
   of royal palm trees and *plátano* a *sonero*
montuno, that song on lovers' lips—a departure
   from this place in which roots hold you down.
A banyan tree with arm-thick vines cannot move;
   instead it chooses to send out more of its sons
into the ground. A crow knows this secret
   history of longing, of solitude—the way a conch
washes up on shore, in it the voices of those who've
   drowned in this desperate crossing to freedom.

   The old man worries about two things: his ancient
books and his daughter, not necessarily in that order,
   though without his books, the old man would have
died long ago. Books of ages' wisdom, the history
   of red foible, this blood that courses deep under
ground. When he speaks of "indulgence," ask
   Caliban, the bearer of firewood, ask him about
this riddle of cuts and bruises, an infinity of tinged
   marks on his hands—ask him for the broken promises,
in this island of stolen dreams, shattered lives.

At night the bullfrogs emerge from the lips
   of ponds, they search for one another as though
to keep count, a record of these nuptial visitations—
   is this indulgence? A man in love with a woman
he could never possess? How he's trained his ear
   to listen to the small sounds she makes inside
this decrepit old mansion, not knowing outside
   her window a man longs for her white presence—
anything, anything at all that reminds him of her,
   a lock of hair, the smell of her clothes set out to dry,

a faint aroma of her passing through.
In the fatal hours of the night, who could resist
such beckoning? The moon hangs low over
the vastness of ocean, not a clue or answer in its pale
abandon. Waves will do the business of waves,
since the beginning of this fated history. Caliban
sits and ponders the nature of love; beneath his naked,
scarred feet the island breathes, rises, falls on all that
cannot be forgotten, ignored, or erased. In the distance,
the drums he hears are not tin, but rather the hollow,

deep-thudded pangs of his own dark passions raging
like a storm cloud about to burst.

FORECAST

As a child he learned to read sunlight, the way shadows cut
   across the sand, a particular hue on the water, a reflection
in the underbellies of clouds, cirrus, purpled like a dead man's

   tongue, a wisp of wind on palm fronds. Then he remembered last
year's storms, how water surged and broke through rock, wood plowed
   through with debris, drowned animals bloated

like sacks of flour, fur pillows, eyes the color of bone moths.
   There went the roofs of thatched huts, dandelions in wind,
water flowed through the village taking with it the memory

   of paths, roads, a travesty of broken logs, branches, fence
posts, clapboard walls. Pigs herded onto a floating barn roof,
   a goat bleated from a church's tower. Nobody listened

when he told them of the impending storm, this inclement weather,
   how rain pelted the earth, pockmarked its own calligraphy
upon everything. One-hundred-fifty-mile-an-hour winds plucked palm trees

   like fingers, sent them sailing into the hillsides. Lightning
cracked the sky into eggshells, broke into the villagers' skin,
   planted there an idea of disaster. Caliban hid in his cave,

observed as ink-black clouds moved over the land, an ominous
   blanket over the world unlike any he'd ever seen. "*Este es el
final,*" he said, "*el mundo se acaba.*" He pondered cliffs, mud

   slides, erasure of land, like some leviathan plunging into the
deep ocean in order to cleanse its own barnacle-
   ridden skin. For days it rained and the world was a filthy

ashen sea, nothing could hold down any longer, afloat, lost,
   the wind spoke its torment inside cave walls,
heeded Caliban's own warnings.

MIRANDA, *NIÑA DE OJOS AZULES*

Mercurial light bleaches the shoreline, hazes
a horizon turned golden by a rising sun,
Caliban marches, heavy-footed with bundled

wood weight, splinters and knobs scraping raw
his shoulders, the back of his neck, deliverer
of saddest news—now he knows nothing

changes in this so-called paradise, a man driven
by his desires for a woman, her father, white
mole as he calls the old man who speaks gibberish,

"Nurture can never stick: on whom my pains,
Humanly taken, all, all lost, quite lost!
And as with age his body uglier grows,

So his mind cankers. I will plague them all,"
and Caliban each morning drops off a load
of wood, leaves it by the kitchen door,

walks around the house to a bedroom window,
watches Miranda sleep or linger in front of her
vanity smoothing silken hair, her divine face moon-

like on the mirror, and he feels himself
crumble, piece by piece, become one with mud,
leaves, grass, back where he belongs.

His loneliness, his own shadow beckons him
forward, an embrace, a kiss, like this undoing
on a daily basis, he's come to rely upon:

one last tempest, enough to drown the world.

EN EL JARDÍN DE LOS ESPEJOS QUEBRADOS, CALIBAN CATCHES A GLIMPSE OF HIS REFLECTION

To call a man a beast, one must see into his heart,
this much he knows is true in this garden of shadow
and light. When he cuts through it, leaving tracks

on the bone-white sands, he often stops to catch
his breath, rest from the day's delivery of wood
to Prospero's house. He thinks of the old man's

daughter, her feather-soft hands, the way she'll smile
up at her dresser mirror, as if she knows this secret
of slatted images on a pond's surface. He hunches

close to the ground, where the warmth from the day's
heat coils about his naked, swollen feet. He feels
his scarred face, this empty promise of healing.

*Yo soy el hombre sin rumbo, el hombre en las tinieblas
de los días y las noches* . . . aimless and uprooted,
the way a porpoise frolics on the crest of the waves,

a manatee's weight sinks it into the wavering penumbra
of a river's depth. Fourteen scars on his scalp, his fingers
know the story, each welt, the piece of his right ear

missing, sliver of cartilage, a nose broken too often.
How could he be the man in love with such a woman?
"*¿Por qué no?*" he calls out. In this island of all things

broken, shifted, he isn't the only one damaged by history,
by the way storms surge and ravage, uprooted royal
palms everywhere, roof shingles like buried hands,

so red, so blue, to call this man a beast you must bow.

LA TEMPESTAD DE LAS PALABRAS BLANCAS

In this island, the saying goes, *cuando llueve,*
llueve a cántaros. The villagers prepare

by simply tying everything down, thatched-
hut roofs, animals, pet parrots are brought

inside. When the storm surges inland, Caliban
studies it from inside his own hut. Three days

of rain now gush down from angry skies,
even the frogs drown hidden in the V's of plantain

fronds, hushed in their final hour of surrender.
No respite, even for the quiet, the broken, the ugly

like this man on a hammock, under a leaking roof,
his life like all these leaks, seeping away, hour

by hour, this lamentation of those island-bound,
not even this physical storm can piece together,

cuando un hombre quiere a una mujer, the wind
blows out the candles, hushes the living's despair.

At night the wind hums through bamboo shutters,
bangs a door or two shut, opens cupboards,

rattles ancient china. In his chest, he hears thunder,
this restless gallop of stallions broken in, *domados.*

En las tinieblas de la noche, el corazón se espanta.

PROSPERO'S PAPERMAKING RECIPE

when making the paper, never talk, good paper is made
      in complete quietness of the mind   a fly buzzes trapped in a
                           lampshade

hands and fingers spread the pulp evenly,
      the act is in total rhythm with the body   a hummingbird
                     pierces a flower

left hand picks up the *su* (bamboo mat)   the children dream of
         leaves fallen backward
            onto the branches

when releasing the *su,* hold it at a 90-degree angle
      to avoid making bubbles   breath is the first wind
           of a storm

hold the *geta* (wood papermaking mold) with a tiger grip,
      but with a flexible hand and wrist that follows

         the motion   a bucket falls into a deep well,
               its sound echoes,
          a tympanum of rung bells

birds flocked on the rice fields scattershot heavenward,
      when they reach the clouds   the paper, the world,
            complete.

HOW THE DAYS GO IN THE TROPICS

At the Last-Stop-Before-Land Bar, the boy dives
for the tourists. They throw in coins, he fetches

them from the sandy bottom of the sea, eyes
cut through the opaline water. His skin is a map

of peels, sunburn, a lost language of ache
and abandonment; just when he's come up,

another coin gets tossed in, and his days relay
into each other, and sometimes to give tourists

a good scare, he stays down for what seems
like five minutes, his lungs tight as fists in his chest,

he counts and counts and looks up through
so much water at the sky, a broken mirror

that promises rain. Only when it rains does
he rest on a hammock in the back of the bar,

where the fish carcasses pile and the feral cats
fight for the scraps. Here he dreams of steady

hard-pressed land where everything is plentiful,
where the wind blows without any trace of salt,

where the birdsong flutters in the foliage
of the trees and insects form halos in the light

of candles, not enough time to miss his role
as a go-between, a translator for the bottom

and the surface of this constant longing.

THE ALCHEMY OF SELF-IMPLOSION

for my father

Once the filament breaks in the heart,
like in a light bulb, you cannot repair it.

Blood stops dead in its tracks. A glass
house cannot withstand the weight

of a lover's breath. It crumbles with desire
and cannot be resurrected from the ashes

of the forsakened. It is an inward spiral,
shards of longing like forget-me-nots

trampled by spotted horses out to graze.
Wood burns unevenly. His eyes close finally,

a curtain drawn to keep out light,
configured to puzzle even surgeons.

A mitral valve cannot be coaxed by shock,
no electric current works at revival.

All that remains is for the hand to plunge
to the heart, rip it out, and massage it.

It becomes a divining rod held backward,
pointed at a crescent moon, black crows flock

into oblivion, eclipse this life's sun.

THE KALEIDOSCOPIC NATURE OF IRASCIBLE PALMS

On cooler nights he builds a *fogata,* sits by it, and nods off
to dream of castoffs. He once read in a book how the prince
of India buried his bride-to-be in a mound of rice, how they
frolicked until harvest. It's one thing to live alone, another

to live with so much yearning. In this island of nocturnal
breeze, he turns into an insomniac, takes walks along the beach
where the dark waves tumble in quiet, a frothy hiss about his
naked feet. On moonless nights, the rock jetties turn

to mammoths, these shapes he's never seen before. What drives
him away from sleep isn't the exhaustion of daily work,
but the constancy of his passion for the old man's daughter, his
inability to simply say, "*Te quiero. Te adoro.*" In Spanish it

sounds too corny. In English too direct, so here he is awake
in the middle of the morning. When the full moon shines its
light against the waves, he can see the bats coming down
from the hillsides to feed on the blossoms of the hibiscus

flowers, the gardenias, these nectar-drinkers. Perched
from the royal palm fronds, they become rotten fruit, dangled
broken promises, unrequited love, all that sinks below
the horizon and never surfaces again, this life of crazy longing.

When he cannot walk farther, Caliban plunges in and lets waves
carry him out; each time he dreams there is no return from such
journeys, such long, painful sorties to love, to madness, this
purgatory he's inherited from the living and the ravaged.

CARBONERO

He brings wood to the old man's house every day,
  watches as the old man's hands tremble,
his thick British accent, his burnt, ocher eyes,

the frailty of his frame, and behind the old man,
  his daughter, fair-skinned, virginal, like in the wood
bearer's dream when he holds her and she isn't even

repelled by his scent of tree sap and fish carcass,
  carbonero him, maker of charcoal which he sells
by the pound door-to-door, whistling a love song

as he goes, and they make eye contact, the old man's
  daughter and him, the radiance of her simple flower
dresses, graceful in how she leans against the doorframe,

light bursts forth behind her, this golden apparition
  that keeps him coming back, in this god-forsaken
island where everyone is a prisoner, where love

burns holes through the palms of his hands, glows.

PROSPERO IN HAVANA

Given to bouts of melancholia, the tempest-raiser
spends time in the garden, picking hibiscus

with the gentlest touch of his fingers, unsteady
in this old age, arthritic, eyes burned-on-the-page

from so much reading, the old books stacked
around the walls of his clapboard shack, the poets

come from all over the island to borrow paper,
which the old man makes for them, recycles,

the vats of paper pulp fertile breeding ground
for the mosquitos that bite his thin exposed legs,

the wounds fester from his constant scratching.
He misses his daughter, and at night he sighs

and curses the darkness. By candlelight he reads
his ancient texts, tries to find order in the minute,

the mundane. The natives call him *El mago blanco*
because of his paper magic, the way he watches

the storms roll inland, like an illusion of dream,
from chaos to creation, from reality to realization,

this *tempestad* of time, how he can make seconds flow
as sand dropping backward into the hourglass,

to be possessed, this alchemy of desire so far, so near.

BLACK CUBAN

Be not afeard: the isle is full of noises,
sounds and sweet airs that give delight.
—Caliban

If you agree that by battering an old man's skull
    you release a flock of crows, like bad words, like
bad omens, then you best not do it, though you
    are quite capable of doing it. The idea of violence
is always present in your worn hands, tinged
    with the possibility of destruction, and why not?
One breath and flies tumble into empty pitchers,
    warped glass reflects hideous faces. Drive a stake
through the old man's heart, why don't you?
    Put him out of his misery, him with his worn
books, his neat, steady hands—the look of death
    in his eyes. Whatever the white man touches turns
to dust, that much is true. Do not be afraid, child,
    the sounds you hear are made by the wind, ravaged
island, the fate of the broken. When the last page
    turns, the old man dies, then there will be a feast,
one big cookout on the sand, a celebration of lust,
    all that is held back will be loose, taken, returned.
Delight in the sounds of one gourd calling another.
    In the horizon, the flock of crows returns home.

STORM HOUSE

The rain falls on the corrugated tin roof, a celestial Morse code tapped out in a downpour, first soft, then resonant. Its echo reverberates inside the walls of the small house, slightly bent on a hillside, overlooking the bay. Its caretaker, known simply as *El que se quedó,* The Stayer, sleeps in the middle of the hard packed dirt floor. He watches the flecks and motes descend slowly over him, like the snow he's never seen. In the corner, the loose tendrils of cobweb bow into *W*'s in the slight breeze brought on by the storm. *Velas,* he thinks, sails. No, the bloated remains of man-o'-wars strewn on the sandy flats during low tide. He never yearns for any other place. He can't recall where he was born, how old he is. He feels ancient already, wrapped in this blanket of moisture and shadow. Storm watcher is he. The rain speaks to him in a lover's language. He grips the dirt beneath his hands and thinks of dust. The rain says *agua.* He says *semilla.* In this arid terrain, between them grows a fertile language of seeds.

BLACK CALLIGRAPHY

The way his fingers callous after carrying so much wood
to Prospero's house—anything for another glimpse
    of his lovely, fair daughter.

A broom closet door open, an empty mouth, dark, damp,
except for all the shoes hung from the ceiling rafters
   like bats, a single lace dangled in memory.

Scars on his back, flashed in a broken mirror, a map
of his fears, a seduction of moonlight upon a banister;
    when will he be loved? Nurtured?

Under his fingernails, a splinter, dug deep, infected,
try as he may with his teeth, he only bites off more flesh,
   a little blood beads on his fingertips.

But this is not about fingers, he thinks, or about nails,
but most certainly about his desire, how he yearns
    for a kiss, a touch, a desperate tug

into this land of the living. Once he arrived home
and found a flock of red-headed vultures perched
   on trees, wings outstretched

on the ground, some pecking out a carcass, slivers
of meat, these last morsels, and when he approached
    them, some took flight, a whack-whack

of wings, beating against their own heaviness, gorged,
he thought, upon the dying of another. One bird
   eyed him, opened its beak, in it a promise

of this solitude upon this island of forgetting, what
rises, must suffer, must die, and Caliban, afraid,
    picks up a stick, a stone, makes noise

the birds take flight, a whirlwind of dust, debris,
memories of all unrequited love, what really hurts
    most men. Soon enough, feathers tumble

like black snow upon the land, spelling out the way.

DESIRE

Among the rubble,
    Caliban's hands blister, turn dark like wings of crow,

tend to wood turned
    charcoal, this modus operandi in the tropics where winds

sift palm fronds, scatter
    paper like *jaibas* across rooms in empty pavilions,

when rain falls, leaks gush
    through gaping wounds, broken tiles on stairways,

cracked lines on walls, floors,
    in the roof, among the distant chatter of parrots and birds

of paradise, Caliban too ponders chaos,
    how every star is a sun that crackles his skin, blisters

it to the size of coins,
    among breaking waves, against a rocky shore, Caliban

studies nature, wingless insects, beetles
    like scabs on red earth, a horseshoe crab's insistent

return to lay eggs
    during low tide, a cut on the meaty leaf of an agave plant,

two names: his and hers, a milky
    secretion on the lacerated skin, a way to leave a record

on this god-forsaken land
    and when rains and storms and plunder come, all creatures

ready themselves
    for water and are unhinged, unstuck, lost.

RULES OF ORDER

the world is written on the flight
    feathers of a raven, iridescent smooth,

how the sun shimmers on a pond's
    surface, carp gulp down air, release

it, each fall the whirl of leaves
    spells out some nature secret

against the banks of brooks and ravines,
    some steamy riddle of mist

after a long, hard rain, a guacamayo
    cries forlorn from the unseen green,

if it calls three times, there will be a good
    harvest, if it cries only once,

the world will live in verdant shadows,
    what is hidden cannot be revealed,

what is taken must be given back,
    placed from where it was plucked,

the inside of a coconut's shell
    holds more than water, a lover's

language for that which is past
    and that which pours forward.

THE RECONCILIATION BETWEEN *LOS QUE SE FUERON*
Y LOS QUE SE QUEDARON

It's an old story in this Caribbean island, how some leave
and others stay. What is exchanged between the villagers?

This gift of words. A storm or two. In the old man's books,
the story has to do with a man who fell from his roof, fell

to pieces, and when the dictator's horses and the dictator's
men couldn't put *el hombre* back together again, the children

gathered at the lip of the beach to lay down hibiscus-blossom
wreaths. This is true of the story of the man who fell out

of the sky, the great revolutionary man, who crashed in a Cessna,
and now schoolchildren sing songs to him, or the Argentinian

who spoke many languages, who had been a medical student
in Buenos Aires, who came to this island to fight for freedom.

Where is he now? When the *zun-zun* hovers above a trough
filled with rainwater, we know it will rain for decades; those

who left will miss their homeland, those who stayed will say
there is no return. Only the dead know the truth. One day

everyone will come together, that's true—for now, we wait,
wait out this rain between the shores of exile. While we wait,

we love, eat, drink, our children grow up knowing the difference
between here and there. They will return one day and plant

new trees, replace what the history's tempest has blown away.

LAS VOCES DE LOS PERDIDOS/VOICES OF THE LOST

Here in opaline waters, a man rises
and falls in a truck-inner-tube-turned-
makeshift-raft; this ashen menagerie

of foam, kelp, debris of countless
others who've perished, succumbed
on the same journey—a man alone

on vermilion waters is a sad sight.
Sea birds flock overhead as if to mock
his struggle, how he left his home

in the night, his sleeping family.
This desperate act of final exits, wrong
like any other. Buoyed, he prays

on the thick gulp of water—his eyes
crusty, red behind the lids as the sun
burns memories from him, cinder-

like fists in his chest. A storm rages
in the horizon. Soon it'll be done.
Someone somewhere will stumble

upon his broken inner tube washed up
with the incoming tide, loose netting,
empty plastic bags, gland-like,

ruptured lungs, a deflated jellyfish—
in it a man's secret history of release.

CALIBAN AND THE SIRENS

How does a spirit find its way back? To the castle's turrets,
dark and damp stairway, closed doors? Such agony
in remembrance. Clouds tell the history of the earth's

passing. Here, where the opaline waters hiss and churn,
he stands with his ankles deep in water, toes buried in sand,
a blue crab made indigo in his shadow. His hand a visor

to keep out the glare. Three of them surface and speak
to him of what they've seen in the murky depths between
this island and the northern tip of Florida. Bodies planted

like road signs, signposts, hair floating like eel grass,
fingers nibbled to bony stumps. These are sea secrets they come
to tell from the shallows, no longer able to lure sailors

to drown in their arms. Caliban stands firm, resolute, bent
against this wind of despair. *Why such longing?* they sing out
to him. *El que mira a el sol, sus ojos pierde.* He who stares

at the sun grows blind. Each scale of their lower body
shimmers, golden flecks of light, rays cutting across rocks
and sand. A black bird flies toward the line of trees. A fair

breeze ruffles the palm fronds. It is a perfect, tropical day.
If he knew better, he'd say this is all a dream. Sunbathers
wading like dolphins, each beckoning him to take a plunge.

Each time he looks at the water, a memory flashes before him.
Bodies afloat in the currents, taken on the crests of waves.
It could be him. Them. Those who try so desperately

to swim ashore. In the distance he hears them sing. Listen now.

ANACHRONISTIC, CALIBAN BREAKS ALL HIS
TIME-KEEPING INVENTIONS

Because there is love between Caliban and Prospero's daughter,
fair Miranda, whom he spies on every time he brings the dead wood
to the house steps, there in her room, reading, brushing her
auburn hair. His merkhet with which he learned to read
the stars, certain bright ones as they move across the wolf-mouth

darkness, his column dial, made of ivory with its two gnomon
pointers, one for summer, one for winter. It is the middle
of his life, his hands are bruised, cold. He will burn his Tibetan
time stick, this great measurer of shadows, how they move inside
his heart, glooming the world. He threw his sand glasses

into the fire, drank until he heard them pop, his sundials
he stepped on, crushed until they turned to powder under his boot,
return history to the earth, he said and promised not to stop
until all clocks would stop their counting, their ticking.
The only time left to be kept was the beating of his own heart

in the ruined caverns of his chest. At night he walked
on the shore, his feet cooled by sea water. In the distance
the stars welcomed him, their eternal child.

TWO — MYTHOMANIA DANCE

WOOD

nobody knows its history better,
                 its ridges, rivulets of desire
a constant splintering like language,
                 and when you listen deep, you hear
it speak your name, a knobby
                 vocabulary in which love carries
a thousand meanings, a cupped hand
                 to the ear will whisper back
the mystery of an egret's whiteness,
                 a heartbeat, what doesn't fall
rises on the cusp of wind, scuttle
                 of leaves across a roof, all along
a yearning for fire, kiss of flame
                 as it darkens, gives up one disguise
to don another, energy's charm,
                 a constancy of power, how hands
clutch what they must possess,
                 this aneurysm of what must be spoken,
but is held back, swallowed like rocks
                 held long enough to be turned
into precious stone, wood's gift
                 of history to all things
unconsolable, splintered, broken.

EXCERPTS FROM THE BOOK OF MYTHOPOESIS

if clouds burst in a sun-filled day and empty
wallets rain down from the heavens, we call
this *suerte*.

   If luck grew a beard and came to a party,
he would smell fresh-pressed, right, look
like Nijinski in his Sunday best, or clearly

      when you visit the Chinese
marketplace and breathe in ginseng, the world
turns into prism light, clothes drying

   from balconies become pigeons,
white, fluttering up to the rafters.
In the Amazon a river is not a river,

but a question mark, a hook with which
to catch bus-sized catfish, mustached
arawanas that smile, drink coffee, tell

   jokes of the underworld, what one
fish said to another while waiting for the bus—
this kind of thing, magical realism we call

      it when shadows grow pockets
into which hands plunder for gold. The old
bearded leader has a problem with urination,

   it trickles out of him with the calm
of a masked sloth, the kind outside your
window right now, if you look he is sticking his

tongue out at you, mocking you, look now.

LA HISTORIA DE LA AUCENSIA; OR, HOW TO KEEP FROM BEING BLINDED BY THE SUN REFLECTING OFF CUBAN BEACH SAND

Barefooted, ankle-deep in sand, between the German
    and Russian tourists, Thucydides lifts the chambered nautilus
shell to his ear, listens for the susurrus of the dead or dying,

    claims he hears *Presidente* Truman and *Presidente* Roosevelt
giving famous speeches—*el mundo se termina,* he knows,
    when he was a child at his great-aunt's house, the echo

of an old Marconi radio after dinner, human waking
    and slumber, deep sounds of someone clearing a throat
in the dark—sure, here tourists come for *caramelo,*

    not the candy of childhood, but the sweet nectar
between young girls' thighs, or boys', depending on taste.
    El caimán, as he calls the island of Cuba, is sinking, this

much he knows—he can feel it with his feet, his toes rooted
    in the heat of this diamond-dust sand, stardust more like it.
What do they want from him? The truth, *la verdad de las*

    mentiras? Offshore, he can see the bodies of those lost
at sea, those perished in crossing, as they return home,
    fill those places emptied of light and shadow, beneath palm

fronds, out in the open where the down-turned skiffs
    transform into pale-white bones of some prehistoric animal.
Welcome to Sodom. *Bienvenidos a Gomorrah!* Here today,

    gone tomorrow. In the belly of that young maiden, a blond
man planted his seed, a rotten flower . . . in the distance a
    flock of crows swoops down, perches on a barge filled

with dead urchins, a mountain of bad omens, so that the tourists
    can swim in peace. *Su cuerpo en llamas,* his body aflame.
Malaise of sunshine. When he looks at the expanse of so much

    white, his knees buckle in, he kneels on sand, shell still
next to his ear, in it *la voz de los muertos y los vivos.* Cursed
    land of hopeless cases. In front of him a woman with a Swiss

cross bathing suit, heart-red in brightness, asking in a foreign
    tongue for salvation, his or hers? At her feet, the history
of absence. She places quarters over his closed eyes, not enough

    fare for passage. Behind his eyelids, light pulses, rapture
between shadows.

THE MYTHOPOESIS OF THE MAN WHO FORGOT THE WAY BACK

In this house of broken longing, the light plays
through the window slats, dust motes
    linger in the air, like ghostly paramecium.
The dog curls itself on the mat, a storm rages
in the distance. This is not an island, this piece
    of earth, greened with last night's rain. Sun,
momentary visitor, gathering light in its arms,
cusped so close to its fading radiance, forget-
    ful of its own history of light.

This man has learned the secret silence of returns,
bridged between shadow and despair, the flight
    of the hummingbird, the caw of crows
up in the trees, soaked monks of the branches.
Like memories, he thinks, lost and unattainable,
    when he finds himself alone, he can hear turmoil
in his heart, a clamor of the years in his chest,
but he refuses to give in to this nostalgia that grips
    his legs, his upper body. Right here by the window
he can see that light is passing by.

This light moving on to some other part of the world,
leaving in its wake a penumbra so heavy
  ˙ when he breathes, his breath
frosts the glass in front of his dark eyes, dark memory.

I, CALIBAN, OR THE EMPEROR OF THE IN-BETWEEN

The crisp pages from *The Book of Sorrows*
make a sound similar to those aluminum
   sheets my father used to cover leaks
   on the roof of our house in Havana, a "pop"
thunder like when you take a saw and bend
it just right, undulation noise, a certain
   quiet desperation, how a boy remembers
   the smoke wisp out of his father's nostrils,
a dragon's breath in the half-light of some cave.
How many lives must be remembered? Lived
   in this land of vast shadows, rain knows
   the history of clouds, tells it daily to the earth.
The earth listens and keeps this secret of passing,
footsteps on its gentle skin. There are days
   on this island, or any island for that matter,
   when the sun lingers in the sky long enough
to burn holes into our communal nostalgia,
this nook and cranny of memory. My father
   liked to nap during those afternoon showers
   on a hammock on the patio, next to the rabbit
hutches, the chickens deep in their roosts.
I sat on a little stool and built pyramids of bolts,
   nuts, washers out of his toolbox. I played
   this game of surrender with time. I watched
my father sleep, his eyes moving behind his lids.

I would place my hands on his forehead, like
   a preacher, as if to heal him, and I could see
   the road ahead. How this man would take his
family out of this island, travel the world
without ever looking back, except during these
   moments when a page makes that flutter-sound
   like rain falling on a roof, a man deeply moved
by this sound, a boy turning toward the light,
toward the shadow, a sound that takes him so far.

URBANESQUE

after Bruegel's *The Tower of Babel*

Don't hold your breath near the ruined river, where water
runs fetid, liver-like chunks of waste run off from this city of
cranes, levers, ropes, and pulleys. The commoners gather daily

to measure the newly found cracks on the walls, read
them as though they are some ancient language of rubble,
scrolls tossed out the windows, these parentheses

cupped in the distance, beehive structures where smoked
sausages hang out to dry, half-dead birds perch on sills,
preen weakly as though pecking for parasite morsels.

Your daily business is to patch, scrape, paint the walls
with lime. You, the leveler, the lonely one, bevel in hand,
too used to life with animals kept indoors here, and the putrid

smells of their droppings confuse even bread makers,
who measure yeast by the cupfuls. Destruction's name is
everywhere, hungover, relentless in its persistence.

Scaffolding embraces the circular city, its ruin, a hug.
During an autumn festival, music fills the hallways, you dance
half-naked with people in the penumbra of alleyways, porticos,

under a cool respite of parasols and awnings. Sunlight
bleaches the landscape orange. Clouds crown the upper
crust of this rotting, festering city-tower. If you cough

or sneeze, it crumbles back to dust, ash, eternity.

LO QUE SE VA EN LA NOCHE/WHAT LEAVES IN THE NIGHT

The calligraphy of wrinkled desire,
   heat on a lover's bed sheets, a boy

anxious in his return home, dimming
   lights of a tarmac, the vermilion shimmer

of storm clouds fisted into corners of sky.

   A sadness of misplaced suitcases, a mother's
wakefulness at the bottom of the sea,

   a vigil to all those dead in the crossing.
A clock whirs, ticks, the slow passing

   of time. Leaves scrape the empty road—
what the night takes, what departs, *lo que*

el viento se lleva, la noche, el mar . . .

The night belongs to all those absent now.

SELF-INTERVIEW IN THE HIBISCUS GARDEN WITH COFFEE AND BAGELS

What do you see beyond the tree canopies?

The black of buzzards   a lace mantilla   blue-eyed demons

If the rivers flood, where do you go?

Rooftops with pigs and chickens   pluck crimson from budding
flowers

When you dream, do you see the colors of your childhood days in Havana?

Sparrow feathers   a billowed mosquito net   my father's shadow

What do you remember of this island surrounded by so much water?

Cobblestones like hands below the surface
the repentance of light   on the fronds of plantains
a guayaba fruit's meaty pink

When the dead speak of bridges, what do they mean?

For the silence to break   a horse's gallop sounds
like the human heart

What do you see recoiled on the moist grass? On the surface of the pond?

filaments of desire   diluvial pollen   a carp's luminous motion

What does the owl want in the middle of the night?

Feed its hunger   pluck desire from the hollows of a dead tree

know the living   transmit the voices of the dead.

SELF-INTERVIEW NEXT TO THE POMEGRANATE TREE

Why has it rained for ten days straight?

This is the history of moist   rain is like fire: vast its hunger

How far do your roots extend?

Far enough to cause damage   uprooted sidewalks   buried hands

In drought, what do you feed on?

Dreams of oasis   an egret's air of light   bitter sugars

What is your favorite color?

Crimson   purple   supple blue of sky

At midnight, what reflects the fool moon on your shadow?

The sacred water   hollowed gourds   orb-like fruit

What journeys do your leaves speak of?

*A river's insistence to create new paths   a calligraphy of
                                                tributaries*

Pit or pith?

*Two halves of the same body   hands upon flesh   a heart's
                                                        stammer*

Does your soul meander after dying?

*No, it glides upon slick surfaces   catches its own shadow
                                            flickers.*

SELF-INTERVIEW WHILE EATING A BOWL OF PLUMS
AND CHILEAN SEEDLESS GRAPES

Why are crows inherently mean, always chased by the mockingbird?

angry iridescence   oil slicked on a wet road   mockery

When you bend over a deep well, what do you hear?

*a seed's echo   the hollow betrayal of water   a faint murmur of
buried hands*

Does your silence mean contentment? Melancholia? Sadness?

blue oasis   royal palm trees   the scour of tempest winds

Why is 4 A.M. the deadest, most fatal hour?

an owl's patience   rodent delight   a scorpion's malice

What are the colors and symbols of your flag?

lapis lazuli   a cross and bow   in the heart of a river

When the end comes, where will your body lay?

opaline feathers   any river   by its mossy banks

How do you sing the last song?

never whistle or hum   pronounce your O's as if in a kiss

Who will remember the history of your body?

*the furniture   a mattress   my black shoes   a vulgar
tongue.*

DICTIONARY OF THE VULGAR TONGUE, PART 1

The Book of Fables shows a man in India who has been standing

    without rest for ten years, having been left by his wife

        for another man, and the man's feet have swollen

to the size of elephant pads. Or the man has simply grown stuck

    by his stumps, these roots he's plunged into the ground,

        quench this thirst of being, how a man surely loses

his way, either in the beginning or during the middle, or at the

    end, but lose his way he must. When he speaks of prostates,

        think of doughnuts, of mangoes spoiled on the vendor's

cart, uneaten. You can soak in perfumed sea-baths

    all you want. You can undo ancient riddles. Marry your

        cousin the way Poe did. In Mexico, you can call forth

the *toqueros,* these guys with a car battery on their backs

    who will shock you with electricity so that you can prove

        your manhood. Foolish for sure, but it always makes

people notice, even beyond the music of mariachis. Or you can

    dream of vulvas after looking at Georgia O'Keeffe's

        paintings of irises, hollowed cow skulls left in desert

sands. Or you can swallow bitter coffee, two days old, a fly

    corpse afloat on the syrupy surface, and begin speaking

        in tongues. Ask the same man what he wants to be

when he comes back in the next life and he will tell you: a bar of soap

    in a women's lockerroom, a bad omen, a bicycle seat, a dog

        who will forever sniff at people's crotches during

parties. Whatever he wants, as long as he returns, to stand

    still for another thousand years.

DICTIONARY OF THE VULGAR TONGUE, PART 2

If you think of wine, think of its aftertaste, think of spoiled
fruit, grapes left inside a kid's lunch box for a week, soured
yogurt, polyps, warts on a midget's fingers. The nubs of a man

who's sliced his middle fingers off to piss off the cops. Think
of a rat's ass, a trail of turds from the cheese to its lair.
Flamingos stand on one leg because they have heavy testicles.

Well, not really, that's a lie, sure, but then again of all the
animals in the kingdom, the grouper is closest to us in its
diurnal bathroom habits, how it lets go these chunks of crap

that float down long enough to feed the smaller fish, who don't
know better. Eschatologically correct, I guess, but pure shit
is hard to find. Simply look in a bat's cave, that's guano!

The best fertilizer in the world. Listen to the man who drinks
cyanide by the shotfuls, then coils a viper around his arms,
all along thinking of Natassia Kinski naked, a giant boa

constrictor wrapped around her body. Go ahead, listen to this
wise, wise man, listen to him until your ears begin to burn blue.

THREE — BLUE TONGUE POEMS

DYSTOPIA; OR, BHAKTIN AND DERRIDA MUD-WRESTLE FOR FUN AND PROFIT

Sure, it begins with insults, a hissed word about fragmentation
here, how words are merely symbols, road signs for the blind,

the big wrecking ball of deconstructionists, a brick-upon-brick
of desire, this language of moths driven to light because they

know not better. Pugilism is dead, who said? Watch these boys,
the one weighing one hundred seventy-five pounds, with blue,

red, and white shorts, France's colors? The one who speaks
with a lisp throws a mean jab, punches the color of grapefruit.

Think of any moment in your life, and you will fall backward
into a knot of blasphemy, memory's inner tube, what keeps all

of us from putting a bullet between the eyes. Who believes
Camus anymore? Sartre? Those existential princes of those dark,

dark moods, when even words can take flight against penumbra,
el escombro de las memorias, in Spanish, words as fists, punch-

drunk, let us all become a little nutty, soft around the waist-
line, wear these thousand-dollar shark-skin suits, Armani, Dior,

Yves Saint Laurent, call the trainers, here comes the first blood,
straightened out the septum, rub Vaseline on all those cut brows,

remove the rubber teeth guards, let these boys speak, growl
about how language is more than pain, more than a blue tongue.

CURVED GEOMETRY, A BOTERO BEAUTY'S RETROSPECTIVE

A chrysanthemum flower in the hair. Who could resist?
Blatant, such excess of flesh, so talcum-powder white

cartography of curves, mounds really, concupiscence,
derelict pleasures, this delight in so much rotundity.

Eros in bed, braided hair, small eyes, lips, breasts.
Forged lovemaking on such a small bed, a simple test.

Gigantism this isn't, but simply nothing like Giacometti,
handsome matador, red cape flung over the bedpost

inviting the bull's charge (*¡Olé Toro!*). Goya's proud *Maja,*
juicy portraits, round, well-filled, a shape that needs filling?

Kindred spirits, lovers, difficulty in kowtowing, portly.
Lathered ladies in bathtubs filled with soapy scented waters.

Macho men with penciled mustaches, cherubic faces,
narcotic smiles, cigarettes so cool in their thin lips.

Obsidian-smooth skin, so much of it, the eye fills slowly.
Parasols in the park, below them gauzy-dressed ladies,

quiverful of a hint of sex in the afternoon air, flirtatious,
rakishly gorgeous, smart, funny, yearning for a heavy-set

smoocher, someone as interested in round shapes as they.
Tantamount to this dimpled geometry, a jiggle of thighs.

Undulant but inviting, yes, luringly embellished by garters.
Virginal some, others dubious, of course, completely jealous.

Wanton needs, who could possess them? Here, a woman
xylophonist by trade, graceful in the way she plays and plays.

You want to possess them, their perfumed bodies, hair,
zipper them open, their hot lips, inviting us to taste, savor.

THE FROG KING IN HIS YOUTH

He remembers how the world filled with water,
this silent memory of ripples caught among
reeds and cattails. He remembers the spring

and leap of younger legs, the stealth approach
in for the kill, how everything tasted better
back when the waters were less contaminated.

Those days of grand living, abundance,
how crickets had more meat to them, even
the skinny dragonflies. And love? Who

could not miss those nights of moonlight,
everybody driven a little mad, hysterical
by so much calling? So many lovelies afloat

everywhere. You could take your pick,
or they could pick you. All that pond action.
And when it was through, another season

of offspring, clouds of them underwater,
waiting to change into final form. When
you hear us quiet in the night, think

of me, the frog king, meditating one
last time, asking the moon forgiveness.

THE MARQUIS DE SADE'S ASCENSION INTO HEAVEN

these are the gardens, a statue turned to face the north
wind, a pond in which the orange-burnt-sienna carp break
the surface to gobble up the mayflies, here a woman,

standing solemnly against the ravages of time, one hand
over her cupped breast, the other rests like a wounded dove
on her thigh, between her legs a river of life, valleys

upon valleys of fertile earth, grasslands and marshes, wading
birds flock in the ebb of the past gone tides, then peck
at the sand for horseshoe crab eggs, this nutrient they

will need to feed their own young, then a man, him, the one
with the swollen eyes from so much crying and weeping,
finally released from that place for the criminally insane,

and he promises he will be good, no more forages into the wild,
and who would not believe such a man? Tired of spirit, crooked
mouthed, bent on the idea of not writing, not even thinking

of words, and one look up at the sky tells him, a shimmer
of cobalt blue, that all the skin he's ever touched, all
the lips he's ever kissed will come back to haunt him, to make

him whole once again, in this crazy place of desire,

    where sky, water, earth fester eternally.

THE FIREWALKERS SAY "OUCH" IN ARAMAIC

What matters most is how well you walk through the fire.
—Charles Bukowski

At first it is hard, and it does burn some, no joke,
but then you get used to it, the intense heat, the way

skin blisters, chars, then heals, it is in the process,
the elders say, and it works only if you rid your mind

of impure thoughts, like the yellow jacket's rub
against anthurium's pistil, pollen of anxiety,

or the water hyacinth's sink under the weight
of a frog seeking shelter, or even the *duerde*

of an umbrella left opened indoors. But always
the fire, how fear and pain can be mastered

here, an intense glow that shimmers to warp
everything so that in the distance a crow

transforms into a solar eclipse, water into hands,
air into a lover's breath, petals lapping the skin,

the earth turns inside out, cold on the inside,
heat and flame on the surface, feet like chisels dig.

BETWEEN FURIES AND REGRET

after Julian Bastien-Lepage's *The Haymakers*

Suddenly she sits up on the grassy slope
where he'd lain next to her—groping under
her burlap skirt—and looks beyond the river

at cumulus clouds crowning a mountain,
how wind sweeps tall fronds of the plantains,
royal palms, almond trees, mighty oaks

and she knows she's made a grave mistake
in allowing him to enter her right there
on the hay, driven like animals by the scent

of blood, a wounded doe buckling in final
surrender. Repulsed by his greedy pawing
of her breasts, how his teeth left marks

on her flesh, she allows for her hands, arms,
to rest on her conquered legs, weakened
still by so much weight he placed on her

with his body, a scent of cut sugarcane
on his skin, a pungent sour smell of sweat.
Yes, revulsion fills her. How he snores

into the midday sun, his hat covering
his face, not too far shadows gather under
the hollows and slopes of a *guayaba* orchard,

a mockingbird male belts out a song
from atop a fence post, the female scurries
about in search of another straw, grass, leaf,

all things broken, all things ravaged, taken.

BLACK HORSE CHURCH

"White horses ride in on the breath of wind."
—Luci Tapahonso, "Blue Horses Rush In"

It was raven black, of shiny mane, and the people said the floods brought it
in, burst through the heavy aspen doors like a cloud of rubber-tire-black
smoke, into the church on the hill, kicking over the pews, froth in its
mouth, like the anger of a thousand years, as it paced up and down the isles,
some demon-like sentinel, whatever got in its path, it muzzled over, like
the votive candle holders, the flower pedestals, even the frail confessionals.
The priest called the sheriff, and soon all pandemonium broke loose in town—
the townspeople couldn't believe it, so they came to see it with their own
eyes. Some said the horse was one of the four horses of the Apocalypse,
the blackest, meanest, most evil one. Some said the horse had been spooked
by the seven days of bad weather, thunder and lightning lunacy. Some claimed
it was possessed and in the shadows its eyes shone like red-hot charcoals,
the devil's rubies. The sheriff called the veterinarian, who came ready
to shoot the animal with a tranquilizing dart and was about to do it when
the horse's owner, a boy of no more than thirteen named Chema (Spanish
for José Maria) ran up the steps, entered the church where everything was still
damp from the rain and the holes on the wind-blown shingled roof—there
were even a few inches of water pooled in the church where the Bibles float-
ed like oak leaves—and he called his horse by its name, "*¡Fiera!*" which
meant "fierce" in Spanish, then he climbed on top of the horse by pushing
himself up from a knocked-down altar chair, then the animal surrendered
to the boy's petting, how his fingers combed through the hair, then the boy
and horse galloped out of the church, in front of hundreds of people, like
a cloud of white smoke, God's black feather turned to breath.

TEA MOON'S HOUR AND THE MYTH OF SINK HOLES

the houses quiver each night hidden in the slope
of valley, a tremor-like shift of earth, unsteady,

a shiver of glass and china in the cupboards,
a rattle of crystal, the dog looks out at the yard,

its ears perked, what it knows or senses it won't tell,
here in the Florida Panhandle where anything

is possible, the birds flock backward into the rafters,
roaches sneak into the crevices of wood and rock,

on the periphery of the pond, eels twist into knots,
driven out of the water by either a need to mate

or something else; a comet plunges into the earth,
leaves these giant bowls in the pastures, oranges

and limes fall to the ground by the thousands,
everyone asleep wakes up long enough to catch

the bright light fading in the sky, the wind keeps
its secret, it's only a matter of time before the plunge.

SINK HOLE ISLAND

The villagers speak of settlements on the hillsides
where fruit trees sprout golden, red-orange flowers,
birds the color of regret perch on palm fronds, preen

celestial blue feathers. In the middle of moonless
nights, children complain of this shifting of earth,
split tableaus way deep underground. Like grinding

teeth. Slow at first, you can't mistake them
for earthquakes because there's no rumbling involved,
only the subtlest of movements, then the sinking.

You are lying on your hammock and there's that gut-
sensation you are going down. Like those elevators
in the skyscrapers in Manhattan. The villagers speak

of being swallowed whole. In their folklore,
they have fifty words for "disappear," fifty more
for "absent." The children take school trips to the mouth

of the volcanoes to leave bird-of-paradise wreaths
in homage to this god, this god of sinking things.
From the distance, they themselves, dressed in uniforms,

create a blue crown on the mountaintop, these tiny dots
so blue when they come down it starts to rain. Water
cascades toward the center of town, darkens in the mud.

The villagers say the earth is so thirsty, and they show
the lines of their cracked hands. Droplets of sweat
like mercury, a flash of silver desire for all things drowned.

ISLA

for JK

In Los Angeles I grew up watching "The Three Stooges,"
"The Little Rascals," "Speed Racer," and the Godzilla movies,

those my mother called "*Los monstruos,*" and though I didn't
yet speak English, I understood why such a creature would,

upon being woken from its centuries-long slumber, rise
and destroy Tokyo's buildings, cars, people—I understood

by the age of twelve what it meant to be unwanted, exiled,
how you move from one country to another where nobody

wants you, nobody knows you, and I sat in front of the TV,
transfixed by the snow-fizz on our old black-and-white,

and when Godzilla bellowed his eardrum-crushing growl,
I screamed back, this victory-holler from one so rejected

and cursed to another. When the monster whipped its tail
and destroyed, I threw a pillow across my room, each time

my mother stormed into the room and asked me what,
what I thought I was doing throwing things at the walls.

"*¡Ese monstruo, esa isla!*" she'd say. That monster, that island,
and I knew she wasn't talking about the movie. She meant

her country, mine, that island in the Caribbean we'd left behind,
itself a reptile-looking mass on each map, on my globe,

a crocodile-like creature rising again, eating us so completely.

AT THE INSOMNIACS' CONVENTION

where once a year the usual complaints are voiced:
the sound of ambulance and fire truck sirens,
car alarms set too sensitive, barks of distant
yard dogs, tick-tock of wind-up clocks, whack-
whack of police helicopters on the chase,
a dripping faucet, gurgling toilets, pipes'
hiss, heavy-breathing wives, snorers really,
bad weather, static of telephone lines, buzz
of computer equipment left on like a dead
whisper from beyond . . . me? Silence
is the root of my insomniac ways, my girls
asleep in the room down the hallway,
and how I know there are teenage boys
in Mexico waiting for them, in dirty rooms,
how they'd love to have them, speak
with their tongues in their ears, and I stay
up most nights like a guardian, hell's
sentinel, a mad dog chasing its tail,
and I say they will not get them, those men,
my daughters, I keep vigil by their bedroom
door, and watch over their sleep, how soundly
they sleep; those men, they will still be there . . .
in Mexico, here, everywhere, waiting.
Little do they know I pass through their nights
like a freight train loaded with radioactive
cargo, and I burn, shine in their malice, glow.

NERUDA IN THE GARDEN OF NOCTURNAL DELIGHTS

El fulgor de las estrellas me va rompiedo los ojos.
—Pablo Neruda

The winds of Isla Negra sift through the place
of a thousand throughways, brick kissed by brick,

marble ledges where the birds perch, spectral,
ashen, driven from the matriarchal sea, pebbles

like golden nuggets in the dying light, *la noche
es así,* the night is like that, a silvery alphabet

of desire, glyphs left to the stranger to decipher,
and the soul feels wind-blown through caverns

where the sea's echo calls out for its ritual
surrender, a coronation of seaweed and kelp.

O great fisherman, you with your empty nets,
your crabbed abandon, stirrer of broken silence,

mariner of fallen orchard leaves, in your wake
and passing, words hang upside down like bats,

one million of them become apostrophes, echoes
in black flight, somewhere in the blood lies the map

to this place, this deep crimson land, absence, pathos,
the desire of heart strings and their sounds of nothing.

IN THE TEMPLE OF DAYDREAMS SOMEONE HAS RUNG A BELL

It begins as a soft ping, much like a bee's canticle
    over a jasmine blossom, this kiss of sound
    over the garden walls, trellises, gazebo
where honeysuckle vines braid their tendrils

of joy. A sound that surges like orange-yellow carp
    breaking the water of a pond's mirrored surface,
    one gulp, two hands clasped in prayer, a stealth
silence like the dragonfly's respite on the broken

reed stem. A perfect bell, a conundrum of echo,
    a counterpoint of ticks and knocks,
    the unraveling of hibiscus secret. The *guayaba*
fruit's smile of perfect pink teeth. Contrast

is the sound of longing, the great Chinese poets
    would agree. Here in this island of open-air
    dreams, fruit shiver at the thought of a knife.
In this garden lovers meet to tangle up their fingers

in hair, in flesh. This moan has been released into
    the four winds; if you crane your ear in the right
    direction, you can hear its soft purr, its beckoning
call, a shoreline dark like the open wings of a crow.

WIND OF IMMORTALS ON THE WAY TO *TZU-JAN*

This unfolding of spirit, the earth's process of change,
   how we live our lives tangled up. When the poet
      speaks, he opts for spontaneity, a doing and undoing,
for nothing. You can see it in the work of a female

cardinal bringing dogwood twigs to make her
   nest, laid on the Y branches, crossing one stick atop
      another, a fire ant under the weight of the last
green leaf of fall, how it dangles there from its pincers,

dragged across a sea of ochre dirt, this calligraphy
   of wild grass, like undecipherable characters. We wait
      behind a cold window, looking out beyond the pond.
If the great Chinese poet drowned there, he died

happy, knowing the moon's reflection was enough.
   You burn up experience in this world, soak up the ashes
      in the next, and in the next you rise up from red-hot
coals, a blacksmith's song of hardship. Pound out

a horseshoe, a sword, its scabbard, when the words
   empty, opt for silence, for a glass of rice wine upon
      which you must get drunk, only then will the moon
speak again, lure you to all those places of your childhood

when the world filled with blue possibility, blue stillness.

THE MARQUIS DE SADE AND THE ABSINTHE DRINKERS OF TALLAHASSEE, FLORIDA

When we gather like this on Sundays,
how can we not contemplate the snug
fit of thong underwear on South Beach

sunbathers or how their toenails shine
with cherry slickness, sand stuck
to their underthighs, half moons

of breasts—but this is not about Miami,
this is about men and women who drink
on my porch and speak of past conquests

as though they were simply saying:
*I've been to Mars, I've seen its red, crumbled
surface—no big deal.* And the great

marquis lifts a bushy eyebrow, asks all
of us: *what is next?* Meaning now
that we are all married, now what?

The guys are gone on beer, they balance
their weight against the rails where
the gardenia bushes have blossomed.

We all stand a little shaky under
the spell of such flowering, unable
to answer. So old man Prospero gathers

his cape, his hat, a cane—he looks us
all square in the eyes and says: *You fucks!*
And leaves, walks right down the deck,

across the lawn and disappears into
the darkness at the pond where frogs
creep us all out with their croaking—

We stand there dumbfounded, drunk,
unable to answer who had invited the geezer—
Had he shown up uninvited like always?

SHAKESPEARE VISITS HAVANA

When asked how he arrived, he pointed a red finger
    toward the docks of Regla beyond El Malecón,

where the dock workers spilled like ants out of the bellies
    of ships, sacks and boxes on their shoulders, and he

said he'd come because he'd heard of the great coffee,
    cigars, sugar so sweet . . . and in his old age, like one

of his greatest old men, Prospero, he wanted to feel
    the Caribbean lunar bliss, the sway of palm fronds

against his face, the scent of gardenia and jasmine.
    In the streets he walked as children played and men

drank in the penumbra of *bodegas* with other men,
    aguardiente, firewater, and he felt so fertile he couldn't

wait to sit down and commit word to paper, say
    the world doesn't stop, not here in this island of fire

where the sun bleaches everything, enough joy
    to fill the hearts of men, and women, the beautiful

ones standing on the wrought-iron veranda balconies,
    an *abanico* in their delicate hands, maidens all.

Later, in his room, he will open the sea-facing windows,
    take a deep breath of the fresh, salt air and sigh,

a memory of homeland a stone's weight in his chest,
    and he thinks he understands what it is to live in exile,

self-inflicted, no less, like the one Hemingway knew,
    Wallace Stevens, Stephen Crane, and others, always

there will be others who will arrive, breathe in the air
  and succumb to deepest melancholia, at his desk

he will write: Shakespeare, and pronounce it in Spanish
  for the first time, the words like hummingbirds

drinking the sweet nectar from his lips, a kiss of remembrance.

THE OLD SOOTHSAYER ENTERS SANTIAGO DE CUBA

Tiresias, what caused your blindness at seven?
How you unfurled your fingers, showed men

a glimpse of their rotten hearts, a globule, a seed,
this memory of desire from having seen Athene,

"*Esa mujer sabrosa*," you would have said. "*Linda*."
But she splashed water into your eyes, this poison

of the ages, how you would never be able to look
at rivers, mountains, a gardenia's yellow blush.

Upon entering this island of fire, your words
turn to *décimas guajira,* a minah bird's squawk

upon the lips of men who won't believe you,
a plague of lies in their lives, enough to destroy

them in their minds. Follow the scent
of sea foam, it will lead you home, deeper still

in this land of constant lack. A burden so heavy,
most men cannot bring themselves to hear you.

At seventy, another woman wipes your eyes
with chamomile tea, rubs your boyish chest

as if she knew that in order for men to save
themselves, their country, they must suffer thus.

Sure, you will live a long life, a bloody path
in the wake of so much strife, so much melancholia,

but you pass through with a wicked, sharp tongue.

AFTER FORTY YEARS OF EXILE, THE POET ARRIVES IN CUBA

He smells the froth of waves from El Malecón,
burnt offerings, like a memory of past conquests,

and he remembers what he came here to say,
like any other truth, this gift of soothsaying,

"When it is time to go, go," he'll say to the man
up on the hill, hidden in the penumbra of his *casa*.

El palacio de las mentiras domables, folks call
this place of broken mirrors. In the distance

he hears a parrot call out: "*¡Mentiroso! ¡Mentiroso!*"
What he is here to do is offer a new possibility

for change, for progress. As he labors uphill,
he sweats, his hundred breasts aflame, huffs, puffs,

holds steady under his hand-carved cane, a snake
coiled up his arm. The sun burns behind his eye-

lids, the sea foams more broken promises, this hiss
of lies. Faint-hearted in the wake of such moving.

The dust tells the story. Ashen pigeons flock
to his swollen feet, peck at his toes, then startled,

shoot skyward. This is a tired Caliban as poet, passing,
coming through, ready to declare against all ravaged.

AMERICAN DRAG RHAPSODY: J. EDGAR HOOVER IN HAVANA

He always came to the Tropicana Night Club in Old Havana,
a touch of Yves Saint Laurent perfume behind the ears, a contact
would meet him there and then take him to the underground

gay nightclubs, where the free-for-all made his head spin,
after the *mojitos* and all the bump-and-grind action, he'd go
home with the blond who caressed his face with smooth dove-

feather hands, tickled him on the soft backs of his knees, licked
him there where the sultry Cuban men liked to give *la espuela,*
a trick they learned from the French, that much he was sure

of—ah, those nights in Havana, those young men who knew him
better than his own mother. Music pulsing behind stucco walls,
a light glinting off a chandelier . . . these nights of release

from daily tensions. The games he played. His favorite scene
of any movie was Ava Gardner's scene with the two dark and
handsome boys in *Night of the Iguana,* shot in Acapulco.

He liked this bite-squeeze of flesh, no doubt. One night he
painted his lips bright red, put on a flamenco dress, sunset red,
white polka dots the size of quarters on the ruffles, onyx shiny

pumps, and he danced in front of mirrors, some distant guitar
weep and clatter of castanets helped him keep the rhythm. Nobody
knew him at the Havana Hilton, not here, not there at the clubs.

He loved this anonymity, this disappearing act of vanishing
before mirrors. Silk scarves around his neck, cotton blouses
rubbing against his nipples. Oh those glorious Havana

mornings when he opened the windows to let some light sneak in:
people below on the move, the bakery boys coming in to work
the dough with their rough fingers, pigeons on the wires, a man

on a balcony with a cigarette in his mouth, smoke wisping
in the wind. Holy Evanescence. How many mornings like this
would he have left in the world? How many nights would he feel

this rapture of passion, unbridled, free? The young man behind
him embracing him to greet the day like lovers, the way men
have held each other into an eternity.

ILLINOIS POETRY SERIES

Laurence Lieberman, Editor

Collected Poems, 1930–83
Josephine Miles (1983; reissue, 1999)

The River Painter
Emily Grosholz (1984)

Healing Song for the Inner Ear
Michael S. Harper (1984)

The Passion of the Right-Angled Man
T. R. Hummer (1984)

Dear John, Dear Coltrane
Michael S. Harper (1985)

Poems from the Sangamon
John Knoepfle (1985)

In It
Stephen Berg (1986)

The Ghosts of Who We Were
Phyllis Thompson (1986)

Moon in a Mason Jar
Robert Wrigley (1986)

Lower-Class Heresy
T. R. Hummer (1987)

Poems: New and Selected
Frederick Morgan (1987)

Furnace Harbor: A Rhapsody of the
North Country
Philip D. Church (1988)

Bad Girl, with Hawk
Nance Van Winckel (1988)

Blue Tango
Michael Van Walleghen (1989)

Eden
Dennis Schmitz (1989)

Waiting for Poppa at the Smithtown
Diner
Peter Serchuk (1990)

Great Blue
Brendan Galvin (1990)

What My Father Believed
Robert Wrigley (1991)

Something Grazes Our Hair
S. J. Marks (1991)

Walking the Blind Dog
G. E. Murray (1992)

The Sawdust War
Jim Barnes (1992)

The God of Indeterminacy
Sandra McPherson (1993)

Off-Season at the Edge of the World
Debora Greger (1994)

Counting the Black Angels
Len Roberts (1994)

Oblivion
Stephen Berg (1995)

To Us, All Flowers Are Roses
Lorna Goodison (1995)

Honorable Amendments
Michael S. Harper (1995)

Points of Departure
Miller Williams (1995)

Dance Script with Electric Ballerina
Alice Fulton (reissue, 1996)

To the Bone: New and Selected Poems
Sydney Lea (1996)

Floating on Solitude
Dave Smith (3-volume reissue, 1996)

Bruised Paradise
Kevin Stein (1996)

Walt Whitman Bathing
David Wagoner (1996)

Rough Cut
Thomas Swiss (1997)

Paris
Jim Barnes (1997)

The Ways We Touch
Miller Williams (1997)

The Rooster Mask
Henry Hart (1998)

The Trouble-Making Finch
Len Roberts (1998)

Grazing
Ira Sadoff (1998)

Turn Thanks
Lorna Goodison (1999)

Traveling Light:
Collected and New Poems
David Wagoner (1999)

Some Jazz a While:
Collected Poems
Miller Williams (1999)

The Iron City
John Bensko (2000)

Songlines in Michaeltree: New and
Collected Poems
Michael S. Harper (2000)

Pursuit of a Wound
Sydney Lea (2000)

The Pebble: Old and New Poems
Mairi MacInnes (2000)

Chance Ransom
Kevin Stein (2000)

House of Poured-Out Waters
Jane Mead (2001)

The Silent Singer: New and Selected
Poems
Len Roberts (2001)

The Salt Hour
J. P. White (2001)

Guide to the Blue Tongue
Virgil Suárez (2002)

The House of Song
David Wagoner (2002)

NATIONAL POETRY SERIES

Eroding Witness
Nathaniel Mackey (1985)
Selected by Michael S. Harper

Palladium
Alice Fulton (1986)
Selected by Mark Strand

Cities in Motion
Sylvia Moss (1987)
Selected by Derek Walcott

The Hand of God and a Few
Bright Flowers
William Olsen (1988)
Selected by David Wagoner

The Great Bird of Love
Paul Zimmer (1989)
Selected by William Stafford

Stubborn
Roland Flint (1990)
Selected by Dave Smith

The Surface
Laura Mullen (1991)
Selected by C. K. Williams

The Dig
Lynn Emanuel (1992)
Selected by Gerald Stern

My Alexandria
Mark Doty (1993)
Selected by Philip Levine

The High Road to Taos
Martin Edmunds (1994)
Selected by Donald Hall

Theater of Animals
Samn Stockwell (1995)
Selected by Louise Glück

The Broken World
Marcus Cafagña (1996)
Selected by Yusef Komunyakaa

Nine Skies
A. V. Christie (1997)
Selected by Sandra McPherson

Lost Wax
Heather Ramsdell (1998)
Selected by James Tate

So Often the Pitcher Goes to Water
until It Breaks
Rigoberto González (1999)
Selected by Ai

Renunciation
Corey Marks (2000)
Selected by Philip Levine

Manderley
Rebecca Wolff (2001)
Selected by Robert Pinsky

OTHER POETRY VOLUMES

Local Men and Domains
James Whitehead (1987)

Her Soul beneath the Bone: Women's
Poetry on Breast Cancer
Edited by Leatrice Lifshitz (1988)

Days from a Dream Almanac
Dennis Tedlock (1990)

Working Classics: Poems on Industrial
Life
Edited by Peter Oresick and Nicholas
Coles (1990)

Hummers, Knucklers, and Slow Curves:
Contemporary Baseball Poems
Edited by Don Johnson (1991)

The Double Reckoning of Christopher
Columbus
Barbara Helfgott Hyett (1992)

Selected Poems
Jean Garrigue (1992)

New and Selected Poems, 1962–92
Laurence Lieberman (1993)

The Dig and Hotel Fiesta
Lynn Emanuel (1994)

For a Living: The Poetry of Work
Edited by Nicholas Coles and Peter
Oresick (1995)

The Tracks We Leave: Poems on
Endangered Wildlife of North America
Barbara Helfgott Hyett (1996)

Peasants Wake for Fellini's Casanova
and Other Poems
Andrea Zanzotto; edited and translated
by John P. Welle and Ruth Feldman;
drawings by Federico Fellini and Augusto
Murer (1997)

Moon in a Mason Jar and What My Fa-
ther Believed
Robert Wrigley (1997)

The Wild Card: Selected Poems, Early
and Late
Karl Shapiro; edited by Stanley Kunitz
and David Ignatow (1998)

Turtle, Swan and Bethlehem in Broad
Daylight
Mark Doty (2000)

Illinois Voices: An Anthology of
Twentieth-Century Poetry
Edited by Kevin Stein and G. E. Murray
(2001)

On a Wing of the Sun
Jim Barnes (3-volume reissue, 2001)

The University of Illinois Press
is a founding member of the
Association of American University Presses.

Composed in 10/14 Galliard
with Meta Black display
by Celia Shapland
for the University of Illinois Press
Designed by Dennis Roberts
Manufactured by Cushing-Malloy, Inc.

University of Illinois Press
1325 South Oak Street
Champaign, IL 61820-6903
www.press.uillinois.edu